BATMAN

VOLUME 1   THE COURT OF OWLS

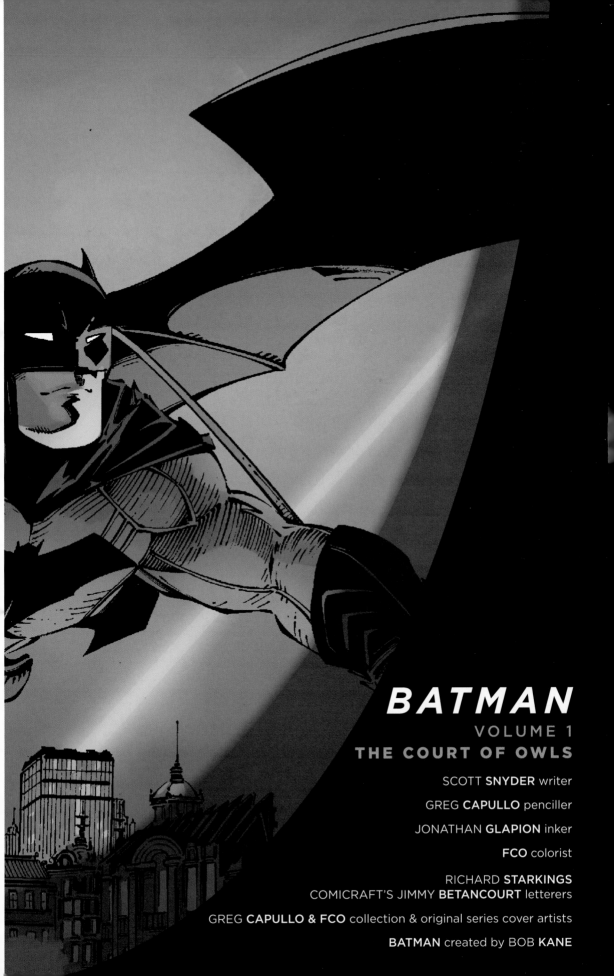

BATMAN

VOLUME 1
THE COURT OF OWLS

SCOTT **SNYDER** writer

GREG **CAPULLO** penciller

JONATHAN **GLAPION** inker

FCO colorist

RICHARD **STARKINGS**
COMICRAFT'S JIMMY **BETANCOURT** letterers

GREG **CAPULLO & FCO** collection & original series cover artists

BATMAN created by BOB **KANE**

MIKE MARTS Editor – Original Series HARVEY RICHARDS JANELLE ASSELIN Associate Editors – Original Series
KATIE KUBERT Assistant Editor PETER HAMBOUSSI Editor
ROBBIN BROSTERMAN Design Director – Books ROBBIE BIEDERMAN Publication Design

BOB HARRAS VP – Editor-in-Chief

DIANE NELSON President DAN DIDIO and JIM LEE Co-Publishers
GEOFF JOHNS Chief Creative Officer
JOHN ROOD Executive VP – Sales, Marketing and Business Development
AMY GENKINS Senior VP – Business and Legal Affairs NAIRI GARDINER Senior VP – Finance
JEFF BOISON VP – Publishing Operations MARK CHIARELLO VP – Art Direction and Design
JOHN CUNNINGHAM VP – Marketing TERRI CUNNINGHAM VP – Talent Relations and Services
ALISON GILL Senior VP – Manufacturing and Operations DAVID HYDE VP – Publicity
HANK KANALZ Senior VP – Digital JAY KOGAN VP – Business and Legal Affairs, Publishing
JACK MAHAN VP – Business Affairs, Talent NICK NAPOLITANO VP – Manufacturing Administration
SUE POHJA VP – Book Sales COURTNEY SIMMONS Senior VP – Publicity
BOB WAYNE Senior VP – Sales

BATMAN VOLUME 1: THE COURT OF OWLS
Published by DC Comics. Cover and compilation Copyright © 2012 DC Comics. All Rights Reserved.

DC Comics, 1700 Broadway, New York, NY 10019
A Warner Bros. Entertainment Company
Printed by RR Donnelley, Salem, VA, USA. 5/18/12. Second Printing.

HC ISBN: 978-1-4012-3541-3
SC ISBN: 978-1-4012-3542-0

Library of Congress Cataloging-in-Publication Data
Snyder, Scott.
Batman volume 1 : The Court of Owls / Scott Snyder, Greg Capullo,
Jonathan Glapion.
p. cm.
ISBN 978-1-4012-3541-3
1. Grpaphic novels. I. Capullo, Greg. II. Glapion, Jonathan. III.
Title.
PN6728.B36S68 2012
741.5'973—dc23
2011051796

Every Saturday, the Gotham Gazette includes a small life-styles piece called "Gotham Is."

In the column, random Gothamites are asked to complete the sentence "Gotham is..." using three words or less.

The Gazette has been running the "Gotham Is" column for years, ever since I was a **boy.**

Here are some of the words used to describe Gotham the past few weeks:

"Damned."

"Cursed."

"Bedlam."

"Murderous..."

MAJESTIC THEATRE

Once in a while, someone names one of the city's **villains** as their answer to the "Gotham Is" question.

Usually it's some kid, a teenager going for shock value.

But now and then someone actually tries to make the argument that the city is best reflected in its villains.

For example. "Gotham is **Two-Face**," meaning Gotham is a city at odds with itself.

Or "Gotham is **Killer Croc.**"

Meaning the city is little more than a **cannibalistic** monster.

...WHAT IS GOTHAM CITY TO ME, *BRUCE WAYNE?* IN A SINGLE WORD... HOME? FAMILY?

PURPOSE?

BUT THE TRUTH-- THE *REAL* TRUTH--IS... I COULDN'T ANSWER THE QUESTION.

BUT THEN I REMEMBERED SOMETHING, FRIENDS. I REMEMBERED SOMETHING MY FATHER, THOMAS WAYNE, USED TO SAY TO ME BEFORE BED SOMETIMES, BACK WHEN I WAS A BOY AND I'D HAD A BAD DAY...

...WHEN I'D FALLEN DOWN A HOLE IN THE GROUND OR SKINNED MY KNEE.

AT THE END OF A DAY LIKE THAT HE'D PAT MY HEAD AND HE'D SAY, "BRUCE, TOMORROW IS ONE DREAM AWAY." THAT WAS HIS PHRASE. SENTIMENTAL, I KNOW. BUT STILL, IT WORKED FOR ME.

NOW, AS MOST OF YOU KNOW, MY FATHER DIED WHEN I WAS JUST A BOY. HE WAS GUNNED DOWN, ALONG WITH MY MOTHER IN *CRIME ALLEY* ACROSS TOWN.

AND AS YOU CAN IMAGINE, THE DAYS FOLLOWING HIS DEATH WERE THE WORST OF MY LIFE. DAYS OF ANGER AND FEAR AND SADNESS. STILL, THAT PHRASE, MY FATHER'S PHRASE--TOMORROW IS ONE DREAM AWAY-- IT KEPT COMING BACK TO ME...

...AND DEEP DOWN I KNEW, MUCH AS IT HURT RIGHT THEN, THINGS WOULD GET *BETTER.*

NOW, WHY AM I TELLING YOU THIS? WELL, FRIENDS, MY POINT IS THIS--WHEN CIRCUMSTANCES ARE CHALLENGING, OR FRIGHTENING, ASKING OURSELVES WHAT OUR CITY "IS" IS *POINTLESS.*

BECAUSE ALL WE WILL SEE, WHEN WE LOOK AROUND AT THE BUILDINGS AND STREETS, WILL BE OUR *OWN* FEARS, OUR OWN FRUSTRATIONS.

OUR OWN *DEMONS.*

BUT IF WE STOP LOOKING TO THE *PRESENT* AND THE *PAST,* AND INSTEAD WE LOOK TO THE *FUTURE...*

"...A BETTER, BRIGHTER GOTHAM IS ONE DREAM AWAY."

ALFRED PENNYWORTH. CARETAKER. WAYNE ESTATE. ACCESS LEVEL: HIGHEST.

WELL DONE, MASTER BRUCE. INSPIRING. THOUGH...

THANK YOU, ALFRED.

THOUGH YOU *DID* FAIL TO MENTION THE MYRIAD OF NEW *BAT-BUNKERS* YOU'LL BE BUILDING THROUGHOUT THE CITY.

HUH. MUST HAVE SLIPPED MY MIND. NEXT PRESENTATION MAYBE.

VICKI VALE. REPORTER FOR THE GOTHAM GAZETTE.

BRUCE! THERE YOU ARE.

SO FIRST YOU FUND THE DIGITIZING OF THE *GAZETTE*, NOW YOU'RE REBUILDING HALF THE CITY...I'D SAY YOU WERE GOTHAM'S OWN *MAN OF TOMORROW*, THAT IS, IF I WASN'T ALREADY SAYING *HE* IS.

LINCOLN MARCH, BRUCE WAYNE. LINCOLN IS--

RUNNING FOR MAYOR, YES, I KNOW. AND MARCH VENTURE... YOU UNDERWROTE LESLIE THOMPKINS'S SATELLITE CLINIC ON THE EAST SIDE, DIDN'T YOU?

LINCOLN MARCH. C.O.O. MARCH VENTURE. CURRENT GOTHAM CITY MAYORAL CANDIDATE.

WOW. I'M IMPRESSED.

-COUGH-COUGH- (LIP READ GO).

I'M SORRY. GO ON.

LIP READ ACTIVATING... OCULAR TARGETING TO...

I WAS JUST SAYING I'M ENTHUSIASTIC TO...

HOW MANY STAB WOUNDS? GOD.

ALL RIGHT, I'LL BE RIGHT DOWN. JUST GIVE ME TEN MINUTES TO ESCAPE FROM PLANET OF THE CREPES.

"CREPE." IT'S A PANCAKE. NEVER MIND.

BRUCE?

I'M SORRY, WHAT?

I WAS SAYING I COULD DO AS EARLY AS TOMORROW. LUNCH? TALK ABOUT YOUR PLANS?

OF COURSE. TOMORROW. ALFRED, SET IT UP, WILL YOU? NOW IF YOU'LL EXCUSE ME FOR A MOMENT, LINCOLN...

The original
Wayne Tower.

If you came to Gotham city today, right now, and took a tour of the building, here are some things your guide would tell you:

The tower was constructed in 1888, under the watch of my great, great grandfather **Alan Wayne**.

He built the tower to serve as a symbol of welcome to people coming to Gotham. And, as your guide will point out, from the ground up, it's designed to give visitors like you the feeling that they're cared for and protected.

For example, your guide will say, the building has twelve gargoyles or *"guardians,"* as Alan insisted they be called-- one to watch over each passageway into the city.

The five guardians at the first tier were placed there to watch over the five original gateways into Gotham--the three bridges and two tunnels.

Higher up the tower is a ring of seven guardians, one to protect each of the seven train lines that converge at Union Station, below Wayne Tower's base.

And at the top of the tower is the *observation deck*, which Alan insisted remain free and open to the public every weekend, all year round.

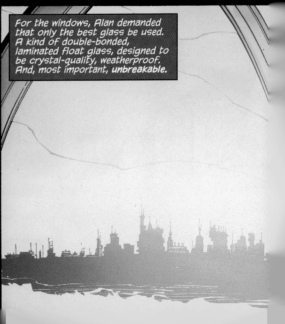

For the windows, Alan demanded that only the best glass be used. A kind of double-bonded, laminated float glass, designed to be crystal-quality, weatherproof. And, most important, **unbreakable**.

CRASH

WHOA. YOU INSTALLED A PHOTOGRAMMETRIC SCANNER IN THE CITY MORGUE...?

IT SIMPLIFIES THINGS.

NO MORE SNEAKING IN AND OUT. COME ON, THOUGH. ADMIT IT. YOU'RE GOING TO MISS THAT VENTILATION SHAFT. THE ONE WITH--

THIS IS THE JOHN DOE I BRIEFED YOU ON, DICK. THE ONE WHO HAD *YOUR DNA* UNDER HIS FINGERNAILS.

GOOD THING WE KEEP ALL OF OUR BAT-FAMILY DNA PROTECTED.

DO YOU RECOGNIZE HIM?

I...DO.

IT WAS ABOUT A WEEK AGO, AT THE END OF THE GROUND-BREAKING FOR OUR NEW WEST SIDE PROMENADE. I WAS LEAVING...

...THE PRESS WAS TAKING PICTURES, ASKING ABOUT YOUR NEW GOTHAM INITIATIVE, AND I WAS HIGHTAILING IT OUT OF THERE AND ALL OF A SUDDEN THIS STRANGER--YOUR JOHN DOE-- CAME UP TO ME AND GRABBED MY ARM.

HE LOOKED HAGGARD. REALLY AT THE END OF HIS ROPE. AND THEN, BEFORE I COULD GET AWAY FROM THE PRESS AND TALK TO HIM, HE SAID SOMETHING LIKE...

"...THEY'RE REAL. THEY'RE EVERYWHERE. AND THEY'RE SENDING HIM FOR YOU-- *ALL* OF YOU."

"...YOU'VE GOT LESS THAN *TWELVE HOURS* TO LIVE."

OLD WAYNE TOWER...

I JUST WANT TO SAY HOW MUCH I APPRECIATE YOUR MEETING WITH ME, BRUCE. I CAN ONLY IMAGINE HOW BUSY YOU MUST BE THESE DAYS.

NOT TOO BUSY TO MEET WITH LINCOLN MARCH, THE "NEXT MAYOR OF GOTHAM."

IS THAT WHAT THE GOSSIPS ARE SAYING?

SOME.

I DON'T DOUBT IT, EITHER. I'VE BEEN READING UP ON YOU. SELF-MADE CAPTAIN OF FINANCE TURNED PHILANTHROPIST. YOU'VE GOT A GOOD STORY. YOU'VE DONE GOOD WORK, TOO. FUNDING THE BOYS' HOME, SETTING UP THE AFTER SCHOOL READ-AND-WRITE.

SO, WHAT DO YOU THINK? DOES THIS NUMBER LOOK SATISFACTORY?

BRUCE, I'M NOT HERE TO ASK FOR *MONEY*...

...DON'T GET ME WRONG, EVERY DOLLAR IS APPRECIATED.

HELL, MAYOR HADY HAS ABOUT TEN LINES OF CREDIT RUNNING AT ALL TIMES.

FROM SOURCES THAT ARE QUESTIONABLE AT BEST.

IF YOU'RE ASKING FOR A PUBLIC ENDORSEMENT, I'M AFRAID I DON'T DO THAT.

I'M NOT AFTER A PUBLIC ENDORSEMENT, EITHER.

ALL I'M REALLY AFTER IS YOUR *VOTE*.

MY VOTE... YOU'VE COME A LONG WAY FOR ONE VOTE, LINCOLN.

THAT'S TRUE. BUT I BELIEVE IN WHAT YOU'RE DOING, BRUCE. THIS INITIATIVE TO REBUILD GOTHAM. IT'S A GOOD THING. AND TO BE FRANK, I SEE A FRIEND IN YOU.

A CYNIC WOULD SAY YOU SEE AN OPPORTUNITY.

THAT'S TRUE. AND A CYNIC WOULD SAY YOU'RE SPEARHEADING THIS NEW GOTHAM INITIATIVE FOR THE IMAGE OF YOUR COMPANY. BECAUSE IT'S A PUBLIC HOLDING, AND SO ON. FOR PRIVATE PURPOSES.

IS THAT WHAT THE GOSSIPS SAY?

SOME.

MAYBE THEY'RE RIGHT.

I SHOULD BE GOING. I'LL LEAVE THE CHECK ON THE TABLE.

YOU KNOW, BRUCE, I LOST MY PARENTS WHEN I WAS A BOY, TOO.

IT'S STRANGE, ISN'T IT? THE WAY IT'S JUST THE DETAILS...THE DETAILS THAT STAY WITH YOU? I CAN BARELY REMEMBER MY MOTHER'S FACE ANYMORE.

BUT I REMEMBER THIS *PIN*--CLEAR AS DAY--THIS PIN SHE WAS WEARING THE DAY OF THE ACCIDENT. I'D MADE IT FOR HER AT SCHOOL IN CERAMICS. IT WAS THIS LITTLE HEART, BUT IT WAS ALL LOPSIDED-- WITH ONE SIDE BIGGER THAN THE OTHER.

SHE WAS WEARING IT PINNED TO THIS FANCY DRESS OF HERS. MY LITTLE UGLY PIN. I DON'T REMEMBER THE DRUNK DRIVER HITTING US. I DON'T REMEMBER MUCH OF THE ACCIDENT...

I *DO* REMEMBER SEEING THE PIN ON THE GROUND THOUGH, AS THE PARAMEDICS TOOK ME AWAY. THE PIN, PERFECTLY PRESERVED, NOT CRACKED OR BROKEN. JUST LYING IN THE ROAD. ALL I WANTED WAS FOR SOMEONE TO PICK IT UP.

I LOST EVERYTHING I HAD THAT NIGHT. FOR A LONG TIME AFTER, I LIVED IN A STATE OF TOTAL *HOPELESSNESS.* I HATED THE WORLD.

BUT THEN I GOT FUNDING FOR SCHOOL. I WAS ABLE TO GO TO CITY COLLEGE. THE CITY SAVED ME, BRUCE. *GOTHAM* SAVED ME.

IT GAVE ME A PURPOSE WHEN I WAS ALONE. JUST LIKE I'LL BET IT DID FOR *YOU.*

WHEN I LOOK AT YOU, I SEE AN ALLY. A *REAL* ONE. AND AS I'M SURE YOU KNOW, THIS IS A CITY WHERE ALLIES ARE FEW AND FAR BETWEEN.

ESPECIALLY *NOW.*

"ESPECIALLY *NOW,*" WHY?

SOMETHING BAD HAS COME BACK TO GOTHAM, BRUCE. SOMETHING ANCIENT AND POWERFUL... AND EVIL.

LINCOLN, WHAT ARE YOU TALKING--

Don't recognize him.

Someone new.

Someone fast.

Just me and him, but still...have to be careful. Restrain myself. Never know who's watching.

Go for strikes that look like lucky blows.

Solar plexus.

Mandibular nerv--

All right. Playtime's over.

Doesn't make sense. It only takes eleven pounds of pressure to collapse a windpipe.

I'm applying over one hundred and he's not even flinching.

Must be on something.

Some kind of venom?

BRUCE WAYNE. THE COURT OF OWLS HAS SENTENCED YOU TO DIE.

Something your tour guide wouldn't mention, either. Because there's one guardian people don't tell you about, when you visit.

There's something I didn't mention earlier, about the design of Old Wayne Tower.

They don't bother to mention it because it was added later, in 1930, and because it sits in the middle of the building and can't be seen from the elevators or the deck.

The *thirteenth guardian.* Installed by Alan's son, Henry, my great-grandfather.

The guardian for visitors to Gotham arriving by air.

Whoever it was that just tried to kill me, he was good.

But he made one mistake.

He tried to use Gotham's legends against me.

HELP!

GOTHAM CITY, WINTER, 1922

SOMEONE HELP ME!

THEY'RE... COMING FOR ME!

HONK

SREEECH

HELP! PLEASE!

HEY THERE, PAL, YOU CAN'T--

PSST... JIMMY.

DON'T YOU RECOGNIZE HIM? IT'S ALAN WAYNE. THE GUY BUILT HALF THIS CITY. GEEZ, GET HIM A BLANKET, WILL YOU, BEFORE HE FREEZES.

They call themselves "Whisper Gang."

And they're one of five gangs that control smuggling in and out of Gotham by rail.

Two days ago, an assassin dressed like an owl tried to kill me while I was meeting with a local politician.

With no security footage of the assassin coming or going from Old Wayne Tower, my assumption is that he came in through the rail lines that converge beneath the building...

...then found a way up through the service elevators. Which means one of the rail gangs saw him and took some toll from him.

The gangs have divided the lines among them.

One line for each gang. One is Yakuza. One is La Eme. Five rail lines. Five gangs.

I've already chatted with the other four gangs.

Whisper Gang is known to be the most vicious and brutal of the five, though.

The candidates--or "sixths"-- are given extensive weapons training overseas, before being allowed to travel to the States.

Once here, they're each fitted with an **iron mask**, symbolic of their loyalty to the gang. A **muzzle** to prove they'll never "snitch."

The mask is soldered together at the back of the head, and can't be removed for at least a year, until the sixth has proven himself.

All of which makes them pretty tough...

THE MAN WHO TRIED TO KILL ME MADE A COMMENT ABOUT HOW MUCH HE "*LOVED KILLING WAYNES.*"

I KNOW THAT. BUT WHOEVER HE IS, THIS MAN WANTS ME TO BELIEVE THAT HE ISN'T JUST A KILLER, BUT THAT HE'S *THE TALON.*

NO WAYNE IN THE LAST FIFTY YEARS HAS DIED SUSPICIOUSLY TO MY KNOWLEDGE...OTHER THAN *YOUR PARENTS,* OF COURSE.

THE TALON? FROM THE COURT OF OWLS FOLKSONG?

EXCEPT HE WANTS ME TO BELIEVE THAT THE COURT ISN'T A FOLKTALE...

...THAT IN REALITY SOME SECRET GROUP OF MEN HAS ACTUALLY BEEN RULING GOTHAM FROM THE SHADOWS SINCE COLONIAL TIMES.

SO I'M ASSUMING THE "WAYNE KILLING" HE'S REFERRING TO INVOLVES SOME INCIDENT FROM THE PAST. SOMETHING TO GIVE CREDIBILITY TO THE BEDTIME STORY.

SO AGAIN... WHAT DO YOU KNOW ABOUT OWLS?

JUST COMMON TRIVIA--THEY'RE CARNIVOROUS. MASTERS OF CAMOUFLAGE... THEY'RE NATURAL PREDATORS OF BATS...

...BUT IN RELATION TO YOUR FAMILY, SIR, THE ONLY REFERENCE I CAN THINK OF IS IRRELEVANT.

I HAVE AN APPARENTLY UNSTOPPABLE KILLER RUNNING AROUND GOTHAM WITH *MY NAME* ON HIS LIST. NOTHING'S IRRELEVANT AT THIS POINT, ALFRED.

YOUR GREAT, GREAT-GRANDFATHER. *ALAN WAYNE.* NEAR THE END OF HIS LIFE, HE SUFFERED FROM AGGRESSIVE SENILITY.

SO I'VE HEARD.

YES, BUT HE SUPPOSEDLY DEVELOPED A PARTICULAR OBSESSION WITH OWLS.

STILL, I DIDN'T REALLY BELIEVE IT WAS THEM BEHIND THE THREATS. THAT IT *COULD* BE THEM.

BUT IT SCARED ME ENOUGH THAT I ASKED MY FRIENDS AT THE G.C.P.D. TO KEEP A BEAD ON ANYTHING RELATED. SO WHEN THE REPORT CAME IN ABOUT YOU BEING TARGETED BY THEM, TOO-- ABOUT HOW THAT MAN LEFT YOU A MESSAGE...THAT JOHN DOE KILLED BY THE TALON--

THE VERDICT ON WHO KILLED THAT MAN IS STILL OUT.

BEWARE THE COURT OF OWLS, BRUCE, THAT WATCHES ALL THE TIME. RULING GOTHAM FROM SHADOWED PERCH, BEHIND GRANITE AND LIME. THEY WATCH YOU AT YOUR HEARTH, THEY WATCH YOU IN YOUR...

...YOUR BED.

SPEAK NOT A WHISPERED WORD OF THEM, OR THEY'LL SEND THE TALON--

I'VE BEEN HEARING THAT OLD RHYME A LOT LATELY, LINCOLN. FRANKLY, I'M GETTING TIRED OF IT.

NOW, IF THERE REALLY *WAS* A COURT OF OWLS...

...DON'T YOU THINK, WITH MY ROOTS IN THIS CITY, I'D HAVE LEARNED THEY WERE REAL LONG AGO?

UNLESS...

UNLESS WHAT?

UNLESS THEY DIDN'T WANT YOU TO. UNTIL NOW.

MAYBE THIS NEW GOTHAM INITIATIVE OF YOURS, RESHAPING THE CITY, MAYBE THEY'RE JUST NOW PAYING ATTENTION TO YOU, TOO. SAME WITH ME.

I'M NOT AFRAID OF GHOST STORIES. AND YOU SHOULDN'T BE, EITHER.

HELL YES, I'M AFRAID. BUT I'M NOT DROPPING MY BID FOR MAYOR, IF THAT'S WHAT YOU'RE IMPLYING.

GOTHAM HAS GIVEN ME EVERYTHING I HAVE. AND I'LL BE *DAMNED* IF I HAND IT OVER TO BUNCH OF *OLD BIRDS.*

THEN YOU HAVE MY VOTE, LINCOLN.

BRUCE, THE HOME FOR BOYS I LIVED IN, AFTER MY PARENTS DIED, IT HAD THIS OLD WOODEN FLOOR. ALWAYS CREAKING. DROVE EVERYONE CRAZY.

NO ONE THE NUNS BROUGHT IN COULD FIGURE IT OUT. THEN ONE DAY SISTER ALISON NOTICED THIS DEPRESSION BY THE CORNER OF THE BUILDING.

TURNS OUT, THE PLACE WAS ON A SINKHOLE. WITHIN A YEAR, THE WHOLE BUILDING WOULD'VE COLLAPSED WITH US INSIDE, IF SHE HADN'T REALIZED IT.

MY POINT IS, SOMETIMES WE BECOME SO CONCERNED WITH LITTLE DANGERS THAT WE DON'T SEE THE BIG ONE, RIGHT BENEATH OUR FEET. THAT'S ALL.

BRUCE?

I'M SORRY, LINCOLN. I HAVE TO GO. I'M GOING TO HAVE MY OWN PEOPLE WATCH YOUR ROOM. THEY'RE THE BEST. GET SOME SLEEP.

BUT, BRUCE, IF THEY'RE WATCHING ME...

"...WHO'S WATCHING YOU?"

Historically, cities are places of superstition.

After all, people come to them from all over the world, from small towns and villages, places they've lived for generations, to inhabit giant mazes of glass and steel, shadow and merciless light.

They'd cling to beliefs from home about what keeps you safe, and what to avoid.

A black cat crosses your path, you'll be plagued by bad luck.

A thirteenth guest at dinner means someone in the party will die at midnight.

My great-grandfather, Alan Wayne, understood the power of superstition. As such, he was one of the first men to eliminate a thirteenth floor from his buildings.

Funny thing, though. To really make good on the superstition, you were supposed to leave a small space in the building between floors twelve and fourteen, a false floor, to contain the bad luck of number thirteen.

A space sealed off from the world, inaccessible. Just a blank slot in the building. An absence like a breath held when passing a graveyard.

A space just big enough--in theory-- for a man to hide in. Perhaps a killer dressed like an owl.

And on the subject of owls, here's a fact about them.

They're one of the rare birds that doesn't build its own nest.

In essence, they invade an enemy's territory...

Instead, what they do is find nests abandoned or in use by rival birds and take them over.

...and build their nests inside his home.

BINGO.

JUNE, 1891

ALFRED.

SIR?

THE FUND
ESTABLISHED
IN ALAN WAYNE'S
NAME.

I DO...BUT I ALSO KNOW THAT YOU'RE BURNING IT AT *BOTH ENDS* ON THIS ONE. YOU'RE WORKING LIKE A MAN OBSESSED--OR *MORE* OBSESSED THAN USUAL--AND AS SUCH, IT'S POSSIBLE YOU'RE NOT SEEING THE FOREST FOR THE TREES.

ANALYSIS NEARLY COMPLETE...

CONTINUE.

THE POINT IS--

HOLD ON. I WAS TALKING TO THE COMPUTER.

COMPUTER--

BRUCE, WE'RE *WORRIED* ABOUT YOU, ALL RIGHT?

TWICE THIS MONTH YOU CAME CLOSE TO *GETTING KILLED,* AND SOME OF US THINK IT'S BECAUSE YOU'RE UNDERESTIMATING YOUR ENEMY HERE.

JIM SAID THAT?

YES, HE DID. THE JOHN DOE WHO CAME UP TO ME--A HIGHLY GHOSTED ID. HE'S KILLED BY AN ASSASSIN CALLING HIMSELF *THE TALON.*

YOU DROP THE GUY OFF A BUILDING AND HE GETS UP AND KILLS HIS RIDE TO THE MORGUE. NOW YOU DISCOVER THESE BASES, HIDDEN IN *WAYNE BUILDINGS...*

...BASES THAT SEEM TO BE FROM DIFFERENT DECADES DATING BACK TO THE 1800s. HOW CAN YOU *NOT* BE A LITTLE APPREHENSIVE ABOUT WHAT MIGHT BE ON THE OTHER SIDE OF THE EQUAL SIGN HERE?

I'M BEING OBJECTIVE, DICK. LIKE I TAUGHT *YOU* TO BE.

COMPUTER--RUN A SECONDARY TEST FOR SHALE.

RUNNING...

TAKE CARE, BRUCE. I HAVE A

DICK... THERE IS NO COURT OF OWLS. I KNOW BECAUSE *I* LOOKED INTO IT.

WHEN, BRUCE? I NEVER HEARD ABOUT IT, AND I WAS HERE FOR--

IT WAS BEFORE THAT. WHEN I WAS A BOY.

ANALYSIS COM--

SHUT UP.

PAUSING...

IT WAS AFTER MY PARENTS WERE KILLED.

IN THE WEEKS FOLLOWING THEIR MURDER...

"...I WAS...*LOST.*

"I COULDN'T ACCEPT IT."

"YOU WERE A *KID*, BRUCE. I WAS THE SAME. HOW ARE YOU SUPPOSED TO ACCEPT--"

"*NO*, DICK...

"...I COULDN'T ACCEPT THAT IT WAS *RANDOM.*

"THAT SOME PLAIN OLD *JOE CHILL*, SOME NO-NAME, HAD KILLED MY PARENTS OVER NOTHING BUT POCKET CHANGE AND PEARLS.

"DEEP DOWN I BELIEVED--I *KNEW*--THERE HAD TO BE SOMETHING *BIGGER* AT WORK."

"OF COURSE, GROWING UP, I'D HEARD THE OLD LEGEND OF *THE COURT OF OWLS.*

"I'D ASKED MY FATHER ABOUT THEM, BUT HE ALWAYS LAUGHED OFF THE IDEA.

"BUT EVEN SO, IN THE DAYS BEFORE MY PARENTS' DEATH, THERE'D BEEN A *SIGN.*

"*A NEST. AN OWL NEST* IN THE ATTIC. HE'D SHOOED THE BIRDS AWAY, BUT THEY'D COME BACK.

"IN AN OLDER VERSION OF THE RHYME, THERE'S A LINE ABOUT 'HEEDING THE SIGNS,' THE OMENS OF THE COURT.

"IN THE AFTERMATH OF THEIR DEATH, I SAW THE NEST AS A SIGN, A *WARNING* MY PARENTS HADN'T HEEDED.

"AND THEN AND THERE, I VOWED *REVENGE.*

"I WAS JUST A BOY, BUT I'D FIND THEM--THE COURT OF OWLS--AND I'D *EXPOSE* THEM. I'D *CRUSH* THEIR WORLD AS THEY HAD MINE."

"SO I BEGAN MY OWN INVESTIGATION INTO THE COURT. IN MANY WAYS, IT WAS MY FIRST CASE AS A *DETECTIVE.*

"AND I WAS *DETERMINED* TO SOLVE IT.

"IMMEDIATELY, CLUES BEGAN PRESENTING THEMSELVES.

"IN A MATTER OF DAYS, IT SEEMED EVERYWHERE I LOOKED THERE WAS SOME SIGN, SOME NEW PIECE OF EVIDENCE POINTING TO THE COURT'S EXISTENCE.

"SO I BEGAN DELVING *DEEPER.*

"IF THE COURT WAS MADE UP OF POWERFUL GOTHAM FAMILIES, THERE WAS NO BETTER PLACE TO START LOOKING THAN MY PARENTS' FRIENDS AND BUSINESS PARTNERS."

0   1   2   3 MI.

GOTHAM CITY

"DESPITE HIS WORK AS A DOCTOR, MY FATHER HAD BEEN DEEPLY INVOLVED IN THE CIVIC MECHANICS OF GOTHAM. NOT JUST CHARITIES, BUT EVERYTHING FROM MUSEUMS TO THE GOTHAM SHIPYARD.

"*ANYONE* COULD BE ONE OF THE COURT. NO ONE COULD BE RULED OUT.

"IN THE COURSE OF JUST A FEW WEEKS, I'D COMPILED NOTES ON SOME OF GOTHAM'S MOST PROMINENT FAMILIES. TO MY MIND--THE MIND OF A BOY DETECTIVE, ALL OF IT WAS EVIDENCE-- EVIDENCE OF A FAR-REACHING CONSPIRACY AGAINST MY FAMILY.

"I'D EVEN LOCATED A BUILDING...AN OLD ABANDONED SOCIAL CLUB WITH A DOUBLE OWL ON THE CREST. A PLACE CALLED *HARBOR HOUSE.* IT WAS--"

"I KNOW IT."

"ALL OF THE FAMILIES I SUSPECTED HAD BELONGED TO THE CLUB AT ONE TIME OR ANOTHER.

"AND LOOKING AT THE SCHEMATICS OF THE BUILDING, I'D DISCOVERED A *ROOM* IN THE UPPER TOWER--WHAT LOOKED LIKE A WINDOWLESS MEETING PLACE, RIGHT ABOVE THE CREST OUTSIDE."

But I found something else on his bones.

A residue.

Dust from a metamorphic rock. Not unlike marble.

Strange, given that the sewer system is constructed almost entirely out of granite.

But that's Gotham. Never ceases to--

HE'LL BE DEAD SOON, YOU KNOW.

SIGGY. *THE BAT SIGNAL.*

YOU'VE BEEN RUNNING HIM HOT ALL WEEK. YOU'RE GOING TO BLOW HIS BULB.

LEAVE IT ON, HARVEY.

I HATE TO SAY IT, COMMISSIONER, BUT IT'S BEEN *EIGHT DAYS.*

THE BAT ISN'T COMING. LEAVING THE LIGHT ON FOR HIM--

IT'S NOT JUST FOR *HIM,* LIEUTENANT BULLOCK...

"...IT'S FOR THE SCUM WHO THINK GOTHAM'S A DAMN *PLAYGROUND* NOW.

"THE ONES WHO'RE *HURTING.*

NO TRANSMISSION DETECTABLE.

"BECAUSE THEY *KNOW* HIM, THE MAN UNDERNEATH THAT MASK. THE MAN MISSING RIGHT NOW.

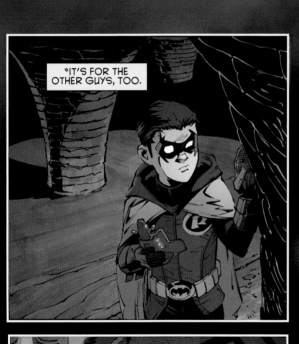

"IT'S FOR THE OTHER GUYS, TOO.

"THE ONES ON *OUR SIDE.*

"HELL, IT'S FOR THE *WHOLE CITY,* LIEUTENANT."

SO LIKE I SAID...

DO YOU ≥KOFF KOFF≥ DO YOU HEAR ME, COURT OF OWLS?

WHOEVER YOU ARE.

THAT... THAT GOES FOR *ALL* OF YOU.

YOU **HEAR ME?!**

YOU CAN'T HIDE FROM ME. I KNOW THIS CITY, DOWN TO ITS FOUNDATION.

FOR EXAMPLE, I KNOW THAT THIS PLACE--THE TASTE OF THE WATER IN THE FOUNTAIN, THE MINERALS...

...WE'RE NEAR *THE RIVER.* AND I KNOW THE BASE OF YOUR BIG UGLY FOUNTAIN...IT'S ≥KOFF≥ WHITE MARBLE. NOT CONSTRUCTION MARBLE LIKE THE REST OF THIS PLACE.

WHICH MAKES IT SOFTER, MORE VULNERABLE TO, SAY... *EXPLOSIONS.*

AND YOU KNOW WHAT EXPLODES? *POTASSIUM CHLORATE.* WHEN IT IGNITES.

WHICH IS WHY I SLIPPED OUT THE SUPPLY OF FILAMENT PLATES FROM YOUR CAMERA BEFORE.

"BUT LEGEND HAS IT, IF A DYING MAN RESISTS THE VISIONS, RESISTS THE PULL TOWARD TRUTH AND JOURNEYS BACK TO THE LAND OF THE LIVING...

"...HE MAY FIND HIMSELF *GREATLY CHANGED* UPON RETURN."

"AND YOU--YOU WHO STAND BEFORE US NOW--WILL CERTAINLY FIND YOURSELF CHANGED...

"...WHEN YOU *OPEN YOUR EYES.*

"WHICH YOU WILL DO NOW..."

...YES, OPEN THOSE EYES FOR US. OPEN YOUR EYES FOR YOUR *COURT!*

YOU HAVE TRAVELED SO FAR, FROM THE BANKS OF THE *RIVER LETHE,* THE RIVER OF MINDLESSNESS, WHERE THE SHADES WALK, BACK TO THIS WORLD, TO YOUR CITY.

GOTHAM.

YES, LOOK... LOOK AT YOUR BODY. IT HAS BEEN RESTORED, AND MADE STRONGER THAN BEFORE. *MUCH* STRONGER.

YOU DRANK FROM THE CUP OF IMMORTALITY, AND YOU CANNOT BE KILLED. YOUR WOUNDS IN BATTLE WILL HEAL.

YOU ARE FASTER, *STRONGER* THAN EVER.

AND *WE* ARE STRONGER, TOO. YOUR COURT. WE HAVE BEEN GATHERING OUR RESOURCES, OUR POWER, AND WAITING AS THE GREAT OWL WAITS-- *IN PLAIN SIGHT.*

UNTIL *NOW...*

...FOR NOW IT IS TIME FOR US TO STRIKE...TO *RECLAIM* THIS CITY...

BRUCE?

I ASKED *ALFRED*--

TO TELL ME YOU NEEDED PRIVACY, I KNOW, BUT I WANTED TO COME DOWN AND SEE YOU.

GEEZ, BRUCE. WHAT DID THEY...*DO* TO YOU?

SO THEY USED THE COMPOUND TO BRING HIM BACK FROM THE DEAD TO *KILL* FOR THEM.

AND HIS FIRST TARGET WAS HIS OLD TRAINER, THE JOHN DOE. AFTER ALL, WHO NEEDS THE COACH ANYMORE WHEN YOU CAN REANIMATE YOUR STAR ATHLETE?

AND HIS HEALING FACTOR?

ONCE THE COMPOUND IS BONDED WITH THE CELLS, THEY'RE CAPABLE OF REACTIVATING AND HEALING OVER AND OVER.

WHICH IS WHY HE WAS ABLE TO WALK AWAY FROM THE FALL OFF WAYNE TOWER.

AND WHY HE'S TECHNICALLY *STILL ALIVE* RIGHT NOW. SO HOW DO YOU TAKE HIM DOWN?

THE *COLD*. THE COMPOUND TURNS THE BODY INTO A KIND OF HEAT-POWERED FACTORY FOR CELL REGROWTH.

THE WAY TO SHUT IT DOWN IS TO LOWER THE HOST'S CORE BODY TEMPERATURE. PUT HIM BACK ON ICE. I'M RUNNING FREEZING SOLUTION INTO HIM NOW.

DO YOU HAVE A NAME FOR HIM YET?

YES. HIS NAME IS COBB. *WILLIAM COBB.*

AND HE'S YOUR *GREAT-GRANDFATHER.*

MY... MY WHAT?

I TOOK A TISSUE SAMPLE, DICK.

AND WHAT, YOU WEREN'T GOING TO TELL ME?

THAT'S WHY YOU WANTED PRIVACY?

THAT'S ONE PART OF IT, YES.

AND YOU'RE NOT GOING TO TELL ME THE OTHER PART.

HEH. OF COURSE YOU'RE NOT.

YOU KNOW, BRUCE, I GET THAT YOU THINK YOU'RE *PROTECTING* ME BY KEEPING YOUR SECRETS.

OR RATHER, I GET THAT YOU *WANT* TO THINK THAT'S WHY YOU KEEP SECRETS LIKE THIS.

BUT SINCE WE'RE BEING SO HONEST AND UP FRONT--RIGHT? LET'S JUST ADMIT THAT *BOTH* OF US KNOW THE PERSON YOU'RE REALLY PROTECTING IS *YOURSELF.*

FROM NEEDING TO HAVE A DAMN *HUMAN* EMOTION!

BUT YOU HAVE NO IDEA WHAT I'VE BEEN THROUGH THESE LAST FEW WEEKS! *NO IDEA!* THE THINGS I'VE HAD TO *DEAL* WITH!

AND I'LL TELL YOU WHAT, BRUCE, IF YOU THINK LEARNING MY ANCESTOR, SOME GUY I NEVER EVEN KNEW, WAS A *CRIMINAL*--

--IF YOU THINK THAT'S GOING TO *FAZE ME,* THEN FRANKLY, YOU DON'T KNOW ME AT--

VARIANT COVER GALLERY

BATMAN 1
by Ethan Van Sciver & Tomeu Morey

BATMAN 2
by Jim Lee, Scott Williams & Alex Sinclair

BATMAN 3
by Ivan Reis, Joe Prado & Rod Reis

BATMAN 4
by Mike Choi

BATMAN 5
by Chris Burnham & Nathan Fairbairn

BATMAN 6
by Gary Frank & FCO

BATMAN 7
by Dustin Nguyen

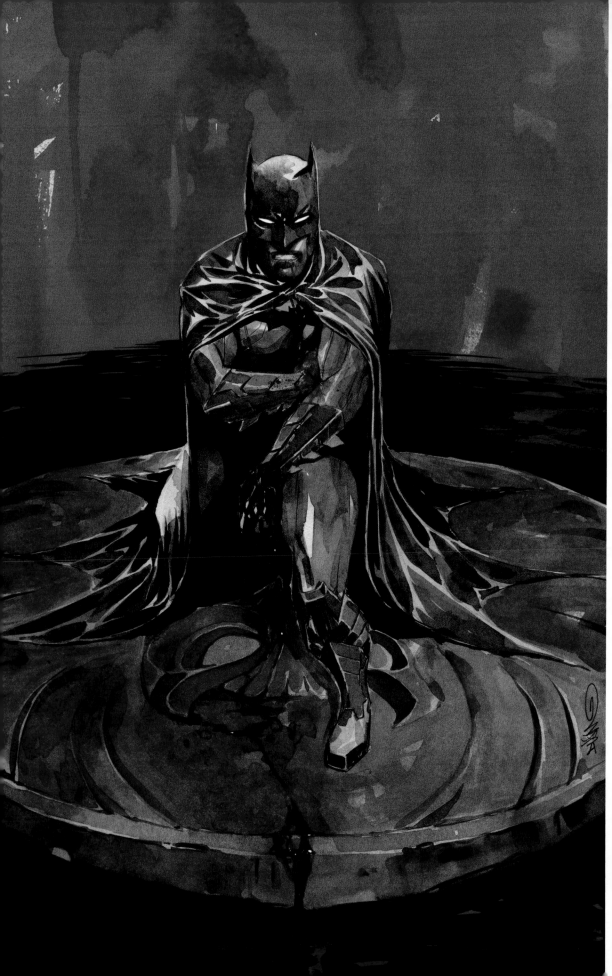

BATMAN #1, PAGES 21-24

SCRIPT BY SCOTT SNYDER   LAYOUTS BY GREG CAPULLO

PAGE 21

21.1
LARGE – the CRIME SCENE – a MAN, pinned to the wall of his loft by DOZENS OF ANTIQUE THROWING KNIVES. The body should be in bad shape – it's been pinned to the wall for almost a week, Greg.

As for the pose, the scene should be reminiscent of one of those circus performances, where someone is strapped to a wheel and spun around while a knife-thrower tosses daggers and always just misses. The thing here, though, is that every knife has hit the victim - all on purpose. So there should be knives in his arms, legs, stomach. One long one – the kill shot - going right into his open mouth, pinning his head to the wooden wall behind.

The MAN himself is a painter in his 50s. He should look a little rakish, maybe a big, broad guy – he was at least, two weeks ago. His loft should be filled with large-scale paintings and canvases.

    HARVEY: Collector friend of his found him around six o'clock. Evidence points to a T.O.D. five, maybe six days ago.

    HARVEY: So. What do you think?

21.2
BATMAN inspecting the body, HARVEY there, too.

    BATMAN: I think whoever did this deliberately missed every major artery.

    BATMAN: Meaning, they wanted to hurt Mr. Lockhart very badly, for a very long time.

21.3
And looking at the KNIVES.

    BATMAN: The knives are throwing weapons, professional grade. The grooves are filled with mercury for steadier flight.

    BATMAN: I'd like to take one.

21.4
HARVEY, as BATMAN examines the VICTIM'S HAND.

    HARVEY: Hell, it's not like we're going to run out.

    HARVEY: Look like Lockhart got a piece of the killer?

21.5
BATMAN, swabbing beneath the VICTIM'S FINGERNAILS for DNA.

    BATMAN (TO ALFRED, THROUGH COWL): Possible DNA analysis. Looks like skin beneath the victims fingernails.

21.6
And placing the flecks of DNA, the skin cells, into a SMALL COMPARTMENT THAT POPS OUT OF HIS GLOVE.

    ALFRED (THROUGH COWL): Running AmpFLP now.

    ALFRED (THROUGH COWL): Anything else, sir?

21.7
BATMAN, sniffing, smelling something that catches his attention.

    ALFRED (THROUGH COWL): Sir?

PAGE 22
22.1
BATMAN – at a wall, looking at a painting. Inspecting. Ever the detective...

22.3
BATMAN, taking the painting down.

   HARVEY: What? What is it?

22.4
BATMAN, waiting for HARVEY to hand him his cigar.

   BATMAN: Give me your cigar.

   HARVEY: My cigar...

22.5
BATMAN, approaching the wall with the cigar. HARVEY, aggravated in the background.

   HARVEY: Fine. Take it. Now. You mind filling me in?

   BATMAN: Smell that? It's linseed oil. A common paint thinner. But the intensity is too strong.

   HARVEY: So this Lockhart guy spilled a can of paint. So what?

22.6
BATMAN about to touch the wall with the cigar.

   BATMAN: Maybe...

PAGE 23
23.1
Large - A FLAMING MESSAGE ON THE
WALL: "BRUCE WAYNE WILL DIE ON
SUNDAY"

23.2
BATMAN, looking at the flaming
message.

BATMAN: Or maybe he was using it to
leave a message, before he was murdered.

HARVEY: Sunday... If Lockhart was killed
five days ago, then he's saying Wayne is
going to die--

BATMAN: Tomorrow. Whoever did this
to Lockhart will try to kill Bruce Wayne
tomorrow.

23.3
HARVEY, talking to BATMAN. Flustered by missing the oil clue.

HARVEY: Good luck to him. Wayne's security has security.

HARVEY: Anyone going to take a crack at the guy is going to have to be someone
close. Someone in Wayne's circle, would be my guess.

HARVEY: Makes you almost feel bad for the guy.

23.4
BATMAN, looking at HARVEY.

BATMAN: Almost?

23.5
HARVEY, explaining.

HARVEY: Look, I know you're pals and all. But guys like Wayne, they don't get how
the city works, the way we do. You and me.

HARVEY: I mean, I listened to his speech tonight on the radio. All about what Gotham
is, what it can be. Will be.

HARVEY: I'm just saying. Anyone who thinks they know Gotham, know it now, then or
in the frickin' future – he's got a rude awakening coming.

PAGE 24

24.1
SMALL - BATMAN, touching his ear, a message coming in. HARVEY, behind him.

      HARVEY: Because you know what I'd answer if I had to do that Gotham Is thing? I'd leave it blank.

      HARVEY: Because no one knows Gotham. It's a mystery. If anything, it knows you.

24.2
SMALL - BATMAN, holding a hand up to HARVEY, cutting him off.

      HARVEY: You think it's your friend, you try to help it, what does it do? It stabs you in the back. That's what. Stabs you right in the back with a--

      BATMAN: Quiet.

      BATMAN (TO PHONE): You're sure.

24.3
SMALL – We're in the CAVE, CLOSE on ALFRED, looking at the BAT-COMPUTER SCREEN (which we cannot see)

    ALRED: Quite, sir. The skin cells beneath the victim's fingernails...

24.4
LARGE AS POSSIBLE - We're in the CAVE with ALFRED, who is standing in front of BATCOMPUTER as he talks to BATMAN through the console. And on the screen.

    ALFRED: Came back a perfect match.

On the SCREEN is says: "DNA MATCH: DICK GRAYSON"

Noose

Riddler

Question
mark
tats on
sides
Q-mark
heircut